A POOL OF SLAVES:
To Be Used And Discarded "at will"

By

Jim Green

DEDICATED TO:

Those who understand that the title, here, is the mind-set used in hiring "employees" in America....in short, we still have one foot on the plantation....and this antiquated mind-set undermines capitalism/our market economy....

ISBN-13: 978-1490399348

ISBN-10: 1490399348

PROLOGUE

At the outset I need to confess something—and that is that I am angry—the election of 2008 had opened a window, a window rare in our history, to make advancements for America—

The Democrats had majorities in the House, Senate, as well as the Presidency—and to limit the opportunity for advancement, here, to "unemployment"—we sometimes forget that fixing unemployment was a major social/political problem on the table—*before* the Great Meltdown....

In short, we had the opportunity during this very narrow window to actually fix the most serious social problem facing America, today—pervasive unemployment—*and we blew it*!

And the objective, here, to describe how we got here, and how we can fix it—will hopefully make crystal clear why we "*blew it!*"—

In a broad brush statement: Up to this time "conventional wisdom" had it: Fix the market, and the market will then fix unemployment—but because of events which are explored below—this was 180 degrees off course—

The world had changed and the economic theories of the past no longer work—but the powers that be in Washington failed to see this and the failure to fix unemployment resulted in a disaster! The 2010 election.....need we say more......

That very narrow window is now closed—but had the Democrats/Progressives actually fixed this major "social" problem—they would have won the 2010 election hands down—and we are still paying for the depth of that loss:

A House, to this day, that is filled with lunatics—the Republican's redistricting that will take until 2020 [our next Census] to root out the extremists currently driving the Republican Party, and unwind the damage this has caused to America—and the damage caused *solely* because we failed to fix unemployment—is almost incalculable!

And, why are the "leaders" in the Republican Party, today—Randy Paul, Ryan, Issa, Cruz, et al-- not identified for what—NOT DECENT PEOPLE [NDP]—Decent people don't act like that—Decent people don't talk like that—these are creeps! So why don't we call them what they are.....?

Also, it may sound alarmist, but our failure to step up to the plate in this very narrow window, may have been our nemesis—we may be on our way out, folks, and the paralysis and obstructive milieu in Washington may really be red flags that we are history.....

And front and center in our decline: The once "Grand Old Party" is anything but "grand" today, and at present their sole objective is to lie, cheat and rob to get elected—so they can lie, cheat and rob the American people blind—once elected!

We are a "representative" government, folks—we elect people to represent what is in our best economic interests—but the Republican party today has a single program—to pander to the GREED of their wealthiest contributors—PERIOD—they stand for nothing else!

The current Republican Party has NO interest in the betterment of

America—and in the process they are giving the finger to the "rank and file", who in their ignorance vote Republican—i.e., why on earth would anyone in their right mind—in a "representative" government—vote for someone who doesn't represent them? [the premise of the book "What's The Matter With Kansas?"—and see also OUR GREED AND IGNORANCE, on Amazon/Kindle].

Thus, to come full circle, I am angry because it may be decades before we again have the opportunity this very narrow window provided in 2009--to actually assist in our evolving as a nation—We had the chance "to make the world a better place"—*and we blew it*!

This is the 11th book I have on Amazon/Kindle—I am surprised it is even one—and it all came about, solely, as a result of the publishing world being turned on its head—and would not have been possible even 10 years ago—

And, all are the product of pent up writings, gathering dust over the past 30 years—also, this book, hopefully, will be the shortest.....

It is based on the premise that we have a 7.6% unemployment rate—[13.8 real rate] with a projected almost 12 million unemployed/underemployed Americans—because we are _on the wrong path_ to fix the unemployment crisis [which resulted from the excesses of the Bush administration/the Supply Side fraud perpetrated on the American people over the past 30 years]—

That is, we are applying antiquated and unworkable economic theories—

that do not work in a modern market economy....

And, evident by the projection by the CBO that it will be 2017, on our current path, to get back to even an anemic 5.5% unemployment rate—and unemployment benefits long since expired.....

This is our current job creation methodology:

In America, as well as all of the OECD countries [our network of market economies] it is *believed* that the Market can provide all the jobs we need [and in spite of overwhelming evidence by just looking at the data that this is patently absurd]—but the point conveniently ignored as a result of this mind-set: ___If the market fails, the unemployed are out of luck!___

This book will trace the history of how we got where we are, and also proposes a solution for what we need to do to address unemployment going forward in the 21st Century.

Every credible economist agrees that sometime around the mid-1970's the world economy underwent a major paradigm shift—and while the explanation for why, differs—one fact is not in dispute "High and persistent unemployment has pervaded almost every OECD country since the mid-1970's." [Dr. William F. Mitchell]—and which continues to this day.

The United States moved quickly to address this major shift in the world economy, and loss in employment, and in 1978 our Congress passed, and President Carter signed into law 15 USC § 3101—which provides us with the "legal authority" to create a "reservoir of public employment" anytime our unemployment rises above "3%"— problem solved....

Hardly, and in spite of the fact that this is a Pro-Market solution—the market thrives when we have a robust, employed, consuming workforce—but the legal authority provided by this law has *never* been implemented, and the window for its implementation---that was opened by the 2008 election—has now been closed—and it may be decades before the opportunity will again arise....

And this is in spite of HR 870 [which died in Committee along with the 112th Congress], a bill introduced by Congressman Conyers which provides for the deficit-neutral implementation of the above law—

And the proposed Pro-Market, deficit-neutral NEIGHBOR-TO-NEIGHBOR JOB CREATION ACT: A federally mandated Social Insurance [the same as Social Security Insurance] to provide a fund to hire/train our unemployed.

For a modest 4% of salary policy cost, we could reduce our unemployment to 3% within a year of passage, and also take a major step towards repairing our infrastructure.

In short, the above is a "win-win" solution—the Market wins, and the American people win!

The truth is, however, we have an uneasy alliance with the whole "employment/unemployment" thing...as it relates to human beings—as Dr. David Ewing penned in his book "Freedom Inside The Organization"

1978 "Employee rights are like a black hole in space, so impacted by tradition that light can barely escape" –

In short, when we speak of employment we think of something a person applies for with hat in hand, rather than from the side of the applicant...and the recognition that being a productive member of society must be a "legal right", a birthright if you will—not the right to a specific job—which is ludicrous--our skills are as varied and unique as we are—but rather that "anybody willing to work should be able to find a job"—a belief 86% of Americans agree with—and thus as a society we have the responsibility to step up to the plate to make it a reality....[it is ludicrous to wait for, or count on, the Market to solve this problem].

In short, the path we should be on is: Fix Unemployment, and this will in turn fix the Market—

Rather than Fix The Market—and then promise [lie] to the American people that this will fix unemployment [and this lie is perpetrated by the Republicans in Congress, daily—it is the Republican One and Only job creation program]!

When Boehner proclaims the Republicans support jobs—he is talking about this "magical thinking" solution, above, to delude Americans—it is BS—it is what we are doing now—IS THE PROOF!

And rather than implementing the "legal authority" above, in the narrow window above in 2009, Democrats went along with HR 2847—Boehner's blather—and we all know the result—

it almost cost President Obama re-election—and it would have if the Republicans had not "gone crazy"!

The bottom line, however, is that unemployment, particularly among our youth, is worldwide [see Chapter Seven, below] and in most countries, including America, at epidemic proportions....

The following letters expand on the above—and as Oscar Wilde averred "The only truly worthless opinion is an unbiased one"—so bias, agreed—but always in the interest in getting at the larger goal—the truth....

Finally, a note to the reader—the letters, here, are mostly letters to President Obama/The Council of Economic Advisers, relative at the time [and not that anyone was listening]--not in sequence, and some redundancy [please look for the nuggets...in between the redundancy...lol...]—also, if you are a "typo-wonk"—are more concerned with sentence structure, etc., than content—you probably won't like my writing—[which is little worse than Somerset Maugham—go read his stuff] and a wayward capital letter, here and there, and appearing out of place but used for emphasis—editorial license— so apologies, here—

Just look for content, please....THX

CHAPTER ONE

FULL EMPLOYMENT IS A PRO-MARKET CONCEPT:

The world economy underwent a paradigm shift in the mid-1970's, resulting from the colliding forces of automation, technology, globalization, etc., reaching a critical mass---And since the mid-1970's the Market has been unable to create the jobs necessary to its viability—With the result that "High and persistent unemployment has pervaded almost every OECD country since the mid-1970's." [Dr. William F. Mitchell].

Our choices in the U.S. were: Adapt and change our laws so that we could apply solutions that would effectively address this cosmic shift in the economy---Or, create a prison system [turn America into a Police State] so that we could hold in place our antiquated solutions....

We chose the latter, and by 1990 we had passed up every other country on earth in locking people up—and currently we have 5% of the world's population, and 25% [one in four] of all prison inmates on Earth, in our prisons! We have the same number incarcerated as China, but they have a billion more people!

Further, billions of dollars previously spent to educate our youth, were being siphoned away to build and maintain our prisons!

And also, by applying antiquated solutions during the Great Rescission, and rather than change—we currently have 25 million unemployed/under-employed Americans—and the CBO projecting it will be 2017 before we get back to even an anemic 5.5% jobless rate—and unemployment benefits long since expired!

The truth is, the world has changed, our solution to end unemployment hasn't, and the result has been a disaster [the 2010 election....].

Ironically, in 1978, the U.S. responded directly to the above economic shift in the mid-1970's, and President Carter signed into law 15 USC § 3101, which "authorizes" the creation of a "reservoir of public employees", anytime our jobless rate exceeded "3%"—a Pro-Market solution--the law was misunderstood, however, and to this day has never been implemented [and in spite of HR 870].

Missing in our current solution, and mind-set: Full Employment is indispensable in creating a decent society, while Unemployment harms the individual, the market, and the larger society!

And accordingly, the path we should be on, and proposed, here, is a Pro-Market, deficit-neutral The Neighbor-To-Neighbor Job Creation Act: A federally mandated Social Insurance—owned by our employed to provide a fund to hire/train our unemployed. For a modest 4% of salary policy cost we can reduce our unemployment to 3% within a year of passage.

See also: ECONOMIC INCLUSIVISM, on Amazon/Kindle

Jim Green, Democrat opponent to Lamar Smith for Congress, 2000

CHAPTER TWO

April 18, 2013

PART 1 [of 2] April Jobs Report

F. Michael Kelleher, Special Assistant
to President Obama

President Obama/Council of Economic
Advisers:

Since the mid-1970's, the Market has
been less, and less, capable of creating
the jobs necessary to its viability—and
going forward in the 21st Century, an
expanding and contracting public
workforce is an—*indispensable*--
component to the effective
functioning of a modern market
economy.

Every credible economist agrees with
Dr. William F. Mitchell that "High and

persistent unemployment has pervaded almost every OECD country since the mid-1970's.".

In the mid-1970's, the world economy underwent a paradigm shift: The colliding forces of automation, technology, globalization, etc., reached a critical mass—resulting in ubiquitous unemployment in all of the OECD countries— leaving their leaders conflicted, ever since, regarding the displaced employee.

Eurozone unemployment is still in double digits, with Greece and Spain both in excess of 20%, and we still have 12 million jobless Americans, in spite of our optimistic, but lethargic, 7.6% unemployment rate.

In the U.S., we took a pro-active role in addressing this economic shift—and in 1978 President Carter signed into law 15 USC § 3101--which "authorizes" the creation of a "reservoir of public employment" anytime unemployment in America exceeds "3%"--a Pro-Market solution.

In Australia, Dr. Mitchell has proposed THE BUFFER STOCK EMPLOYMENT MODEL: An expanding and contracting public workforce, that expands during downturns in the market, and contracts as employees return to the private sector, and in applying our Law--triggered anytime our unemployment exceeds 3%.

PART 2 [of 2] April Jobs Report

For multiple reasons, the legacy of fear associated with McCarthyism, the erroneous belief that public sector jobs equate with massive deficit spending [given our $16 trillion debt], and the overarching reason: The failure to recognize unemployment as a "social" problem, i.e., we, as a society, are compelled to address—But Washington keeps insisting that the market can fix a problem—it is no longer capable of fixing--i.e., pervasive unemployment--and appears oblivious to a truism under this scenario: If the market fails, the unemployed are out of luck--

In short, the world has changed, our solution hasn't, and fixing unemployment has been a disaster [the 2010 election...we celebrate automation, but are remiss in addressing the displaced employee].

And not being considered are Pro-Market, deficit-neutral solutions: HR 870 [funded by a stock transaction fee], and The Neighbor-To-Neighbor Job Creation Act: A federally mandated, mutual insurance, owned by our employed—to provide a fund to hire/train our unemployed [via Social Insurance]. For a modest 4% of salary policy cost, we could reduce our unemployment to 3%, within a year of passage [and in concert with 86% of Americans who believe that "anybody willing to work should be able to find a job"].

In closing, jobs beget jobs--and this would create more private sector jobs in 6 months, than our current path [HR 2847—The HIRE Act], in six years....and evidenced by the CBO projection that on our current path it will take until 2017 just to get back to a barely acceptable 5.5% unemployment rate [with unemployment benefits long since expired]—and for not the least of reasons, this would restore and inspire confidence in the economy, and address domestic violence—[and the failure by the

Senate to pass common sense gun control was one of he most shameful days in American history!].

See also: ECONOMIC INCLUSIVISM, and BACK TO FULL EMPLOYMENT, on Amazon/Kindle.

Jim Green, Congressional Democrat opponent to Lamar Smith, 2000
www.Inclusivism.org

CHAPTER THREE

President Obama/Council of Economic Advisers:

Capitalism is ideal in producing and selling corn flakes and cars—It doesn't work in solving "social problems" such as unemployment and our healthcare....

And when we have tried "privatization" to solve our social problems—it has been a disaster:

Essential programs have been cut— such as the elimination of text books from the Job Corps education program—to increase profits, and cronyism has been rampant—

And in our "for profit" healthcare system, billions of dollars are siphoned away from the premiums we send in—and do not go to the healthcare of ANYONE—but rather is used to pay for lobbyists, to make the CEO's filthy rich—and spent on propaganda ads to keep it that way!

Further, it attracts a few who see healthcare as a means to get rich, rather than cure the ill....

The truth is, we currently have a blended system—and they are, in fact, indispensable to each other:

Were it not for Social Security Insurance moneys percolating up through our economy in 2008—we would not be talking about having narrowly averted another Great Depression—We would be buried in one!

Social Insurance is a vital ingredient in building a vibrant and decent society—And, invent a better widget, sell the company for a million bucks, and retire in South Florida [capitalism]—is as well a vital ingredient in building a vibrant and decent society.

So why do we have this war of words pitting the two against each other—rather than educating the American people regarding the indispensable symbiotic relationship they have to each other?

Most Republicans ask God in their prayers at night to be protected from communists, or socialists, or even worse "liberals"—

And this war of words disguises that the Republican Party, today, is not the Pro-Market party they boast—but rather their policies are, in fact, Anti-Market—destructive to capitalism!

Pandering to the greed of their wealthiest contributors—the Republican One and Only program—is NOT a Pro-Market concept!

Another misnomer in the war of words, is right-wing invented "entitlement"—a word that should be banned from honest discussion—do we refer to our auto insurance as an "entitlement"?

And when Social Security Insurance brings in more that it pays out, i.e., is deficit-neutral--how is that an "entitlement", and why is it portrayed in our graphs as a "government expense"—or even included? If a corporation reported a massive loss on a product they in fact made money— they would be charged with fraud in a New York Minute!

The list goes on—please see: OUR
GREED AND IGNORANCE, on
Amazon/Kindle

Jim Green, Democrat congressional
opponent to Lamar Smith, 2000

CHAPTER FOUR

President Obama/Council of Economic Advisers:

The major question facing America today: Do we fix the economy, and this in turn will fix our unemployment crisis--versus--Do we fix unemployment, and this in turn will fix the economy? Is not being asked--

Indeed, the latter is not even on the table—all of the legislation coming out of the 111th Congress, when the Democrats held the House, Senate and Presidency—was framed around "jump start" the market and this will, in turn fix unemployment—it didn't work—in spite of venerable economic theory saying it would--

In 2013 we still have 12 million jobless Americans, and the CBO projecting

that it will be 2017 before we get back to even 5.5% [an "acceptable" rate]—and unemployment benefits long since expired.

For clarity, former Labor Secretary Elaine Chao is immersed in the former, she speaks of "ONLY the market can create jobs"—as if it were fact, not theory. Her mind is not only closed--the latter has never even occurred to her because she is INCAPABLE of thinking otherwise—and it is as erroneous as "cut taxes for the 1%, and this will create jobs"—IT DOESN'T WORK—[as we have learned, GREED is just too compelling a factor]--

When our mind-set in problem-solving is anachronistic or wrong—we wind up on the wrong path to a solution—and it is impossible to still have a 7.9%

unemployment rate and ignore that we are on the wrong path—

Further, while waiting to fix this major "social" problem--skills are lost, and America has lost the benefit of its greatest resource—the American employee.

Ironically, we already have the legal authority to end our unemployment crisis via Pro-Market 15 USC § 3101, And going forward it is mandatory that our "mind-set" regarding job creation, include:

1] It must be based on the premise that we have far more work that needs to be done in America—than we have persons to fill these jobs—[the notion that we would need "make work" jobs—is both a myth, and patently absurd]--

2] It must have renewable funding—
"jump start" solutions [such as HR
2847—HIRE Act] don't work—For one,
the market is no longer capable of
providing the jobs necessary to its
viability--

3] It will not add a dime to our deficit!
Our unemployment is not the result of
a lack of jobs, or money—but rather a
lack of imagination—

15 USC § 3101 [HR 870--112th Congress] is
a Pro-Market "win-win" solution—The
American people win, and the market
wins.

See also: ECONOMIC INCLUSIVISM on
Amazon/Kindle

Jim Green, candidate for Congress,
2000

CHAPTER FIVE

THE HISTORY OF HOW WE GOT WHERE WE ARE:

In the mid-1970's, the colliding forces of automation, technology, globalization, etc., reached a critical mass—resulting in a Market no longer capable of producing the jobs necessary to its viability, and causing ubiquitous unemployment in all of the OECD countries--leaving their leaders conflicted, ever since, regarding the displaced employee. Eurozone unemployment is still in double digits, and Greece and Spain both in excess of 20%. High unemployment was also a major factor in Arab Spring.

In the U.S., we took a pro-active role in addressing this economic shift—and in 1978 President Carter signed into law 15 USC § 3101--which "authorizes" the creation of a "reservoir of public employment" at any time our unemployment in America exceeds "3%"—a Pro-Market solution....

In 1979, however, and in a panic over Humphrey-Hawkins—our ultra-conservative foundations, and desperate to promote the Supply-Side fraud, embraced a flawed paper by an obscure MIT student, David L. Birch "The Job Generation Process"; and [with lots of cash] gave his paper almost biblical importance, and every president since has cited his finding as gospel.

Birch's paper concluded that "small businesses" were the greatest generator of new jobs—problem is, for the purposes of policy-making—it is pure BS. In a study at Harvard University in 2010, "The Myth of Small

Business Job Creation" The research shows "no systematic relationship between firm size and growth." And that small businesses can actually detract from job growth.

And yet, Washington still persists in trying to make this unworkable method work—[fix unemployment via fixing the market] with the results the proof--It would be impossible to still have 7.8% unemployment—if we were on the right path—and among other problems with this concept--if the market fails, the unemployed are out of luck.

What apparently isn't clear going forward is that an expanding and contracting public workforce is an INDISPENSABLE component to the correct functioning of a modern market economy—

The market thrives when we have a robust, employed, consuming workforce—and overlooked is that HR 870 [112th Congress], and the proposed "Neighbor-To-Neighbor Job Creation Act" outlined in "ECONOMIC INCLUSIVISM" on Amazon/Kindle, are deficit-neutral--Pro-Market "win-win" solutions:

The American people win, and capitalism wins—

Jim Green, Democrat opponent to Lamar Smith, 2000

CHAPTER SIX

<u>The legacy of Our Irrational Fear</u>

NOTE TO THE READER: I didn't write the initial item—I wish I had—it is exquisitely succinct in defining a major problem facing America, today—"irrational fear"—that may doom America, and in its malignancy causes people to vote Republican—I cut and pasted it from the internet, and included in this chapter, in part, to see if you are paying attention—I wish the author would come forward and claim authorship...but for here will just say THX—and post this segment as: Anonymous

"Conservatives are such cowards: they are afraid of gay people getting married or serving in the military; they are afraid of bringing terrorists to super max prisons in the US from which no one has ever escaped; they are afraid of the boy scouts letting gay kids in; they are afraid of everyone voting and are constantly suppressing the vote under some bogus voter fraud theory; they are afraid of letting students vote at their universities; they are afraid of women having the right to choose; they even are afraid of women getting contraception [the real issue actually is a women's agency and control over their bodies]; they are afraid of immigration reform leading to citizenship because they are afraid of-- name whatever reason; they are afraid of mandating gun purchasers to undergo background checks for crazy people and terrorists; they are afraid of people smoking pot; they are afraid of climate change being real and contradicting their beloved Bible; they are afraid of legitimate campaign reform; they are afraid of Muslims; they are afraid of blacks; they are afraid of atheists; they are afraid of hippies; they are afraid of socialists; they are probably still afraid of monsters under their beds; they are just rank cowards and keep making things up to be afraid of."

Anonymous

The following, I did write and it is a follow-up to a book I have on Amazon/Kindle--AMERICA IS ONE SICK MF—and I defy anyone to read the Prologue to this book, and not agree with the title—but for those lacking in nuance, it will no doubt be misunderstood—and least understood is that our greatest strength is our RIGHT to be critical—so we can fix what is wrong with us....

Why America is FU!

1] We have 5 times more of our citizens incarcerated than any other country in the world—and yet we claim to be the most "free"—We have the same incarcerated at China, but they have a billion more people!

2] We have a 1000 times plus more people killed by guns than any other country in the world—

3] We are the only major country in the world that doesn't provide universal healthcare for its citizens—Our "for profit" system attracts persons who see our healthcare as a way to "get rich", rather than cure the ill—and which has relegated us to 37th in the world by the World Health Organization—and fear mongering books such as Conscious Capitalism, is a major factor!

4] We still have 12 million jobless Americans—and while this is a ubiquitous problem—affecting all of the OECD countries—we have the legal authority to end this problem, tomorrow, but because of "OUR GREED AND IGNORANCE" [on Amazon/Kindle]—this legal authority is treated as if it were the plague.

That is, we are STILL quaking in the shadow of McCarthyism—and we still have one foot on the plantation—i.e., the American employee is seen as a "commodity"—an object indistinguishable from the machine they operate—and drawn from a "pool of slaves" to be used and discarded "at will"—[this is the model we operate on]--but rather than change—and our bringing America into the 21st Century—we have created a Police State to hold our antiquated solutions in place—Further, it is the fear of putting this model at risk that has stood in the way of our ending our unemployment crisis—creating public sector jobs—and it is the reason we have 12 million still unemployed.

And finally, a major factor in our Irrational Fear and xenophobia is illuminated in my 4th of July letter to the editor/2013:

EDITOR/NYTimes: Fourth of July Letter/2013

We have a dirty little secret that is undermining our freedom in America, this 4th of July—and we need to put an end to it, by bringing it into the light—

Specifically, Washington is in paralysis because of "Racism"—i.e., racism is the driving force behind the agenda of the Republicans in Congress—

And their ludicrous claims of "scandal"—where NONE exists—Except for themselves, and their obstructive, destructive attacks on America is a consummate scandal!

And while not every person who votes Republican, is a racist—it represents a large enough percent of those who vote Republican to drown out those who aren't—

And Exhibit 1, is to listen to Randy Paul, et al., [who are Not Decent People (an NDP)—and need to be so defined as such]....who do those who vote Republican [and are not racists] think these jerks are talking to? And the level of vitriol coming out of the House—with the Republicans talking directly to our "racists"—in sum, the worst of the worst are undermining America!

Sore losers talk with this kind of desperation—when they can't win—in this case because of the Republican anti-Christian agenda—they strike out in desperation to the worst of our worst—our "racists"!

Here is a suggestion: And we should start with Issa in the House, and McConnell in the Senate—and apply it to every obstructionist in Congress, we need to charge them with: Treason against the United States.

These buffoons have set out to undermine America, so they can appeal to our racists—and if that isn't treason, folks, what is?

See Also: OUR GREED AND IGNORANCE, on Amazon/Kindle

Jim Green, Democrat opponent to Lamar Smith for Congress, 2000

CHAPTER SEVEN

<u>Unemployment Worldwide</u>

Unemployment rate by country, prepared by the Division of International Labor Comparisons, Eurostat, and the statistical division of the OECD:

Country / Region

Unemployment rate (%)

Source / date of information

 Afghanistan 36.0 2008[3]
 Albania 13.23 2011 (Q4)[4][verification needed]
 Algeria 10.0 2010 (September)[5]
 American Samoa (United States) 29.8 2005 [3]

Andorra 2.9 2009

Anguilla (United Kingdom) 7.8 2002 (July)[6]

Antigua and Barbuda 11.0 2001[3]

Argentina 7.1 2012 (Q1)[7]

Armenia 17.3 2012[8]

Aruba (Netherlands) 5.7 2007[9]

Australia 5.4 2013 (January)[10]

Austria 3.9 (previously employed individuals only) 2012 (April)[11]

Azerbaijan 6.0 2009[12]

Bahrain 15 2005[13]

Bangladesh 5.0 2009[14]

Barbados 9.4 2010 (Q3)[15]

Belarus 0.7 2010[16]

Belgium 7.4 2013 (January)[11]

Belize 23.2 2010[17]

Bermuda 4.5 2009 (May)[18]

Bhutan 4.0 2009[19]

Bolivia 6.0 2010 (Q2)[20]

Bosnia and Herzegovina 27.6 2011[21]

Botswana 7.5 2007[3]

Brazil 4.7 2011 (December)[22]

British Virgin Islands (United Kingdom) 3.1 2007[23]

Brunei 3.9 2008[3]

Bulgaria 12.6 2012 (October)[11]

Burma 4.9 2009[3]

Cambodia 1.68 2008[24]

Cameroon 4.4 (underemployment - 75.8) 30.0[3] (CIA estimate) 2005[25]

Canada 7.2 2013 (March)[26]

Cape Verde 13.1 2010 (May)[27]

Cayman Islands (United Kingdom) 4.0 (5.5 - 2010 estimate)[28] 2008[29]

Central African Republic 8.0 2001[3]

Chile 6.2 2012 (November)[30]

China, People's Republic of 4.1 2010 (September)[31]

Cocos (Keeling) Islands (Australia) 11.3 2006[32]

Colombia 9.7 2011 (September)[33]

Comoros 20.0 1996[3]

Cook Islands 13.1 2001[34]

Costa Rica 7.8 2009 (October)[35]

Croatia 21.6 2013 [36]

Cuba 1.6 2009[3]

Cyprus 15.6 2013 (Q3)[11]
Czech Republic 7.3 2012 (October)[11]
Denmark 7.7 2012 (October)[11]
Djibouti 59.0 2007[3]
Dominica 23.0 2000[3]
Dominican Republic 14.4 2010
(April)[37]
East Timor 20.0 2006
Ecuador 7.7 2010 (Q2)[20]
Egypt 9.4 2009 (Q4)[20][38]
El Salvador 7.2 2009[3]
Equatorial Guinea 30.0 1998[3]
Estonia 10.8 2012 (March)[39]
European Union 11.1 2012 (July)[40]
Faroe Islands (Denmark) 5.9 2010
(May)[41]
Fiji 8.6 2007[42][43]
Finland 8.2 2013 (April)[11]
France 11 2013 (April)[11]
French Polynesia (France) 11.7 2007[44]
Gabon 21.0 2006[3]
Gaza Strip 37.8 2010[45]
Georgia 15.1 2011[46]
Germany 5.4 2012 (October)[11]

Ghana 3.6 2008 (September)[47]

Gibraltar (United Kingdom) 1.8 2011[48]

Greece 27.0 2012 (November)[49]

Greenland (Denmark) 7.8 2009[50]

Grenada 24.5 2009 (June)[51]

Guam (United States) 10.7 2012 (December)[52][53]

Guatemala 3.2 2005[3]

Guernsey (United Kingdom) 1.5 2010 (Q2)[54]

Guyana 9.0 2009 (July)[55]

Honduras 27.8 2007

Hong Kong (China) 3.3 2012 (July–September)[56]

Hungary 10.9 2012 (September)[11]

Iceland 5.7 2012 (October)[11]

India 3.8 2011 est.[57]

Indonesia 6.56 2011 (August)[58]

Iran 11.5 2011 (Q3)[59]

Iraq 18.0 2009 (February)[60]

Ireland 13.7 2013 (May)[61]

Isle of Man 1.8 2010 (August)[62]

Israel 6.7 2012 (November)[63]

Italy 12.0 2013 (April)[11]
Jamaica 11.3 2009 (July)[64]
Japan 4.2 2012 (September)[11]
Jersey (United Kingdom) 2.7 2009 (July)[65]
Jordan 11.9 2010 (Q4)[66]
Kazakhstan 6.1 2010 (May)[67]
Kenya 42.0 2009[68]
Kiribati 38.2 2006[69]
Kosovo[a] 40.0 2010[70]
Kuwait 1.5 2008 (March)[71]
Kyrgyzstan 8.2 2008[72][73]
Laos 2.5 2009[3]
Latvia 14.2 2012 (September)[11]
Lebanon 10.0 2009 (July)[74]
Lesotho 22.7 2008[75]
Libya 13.0 2005 (May)[76]
Liechtenstein 1.5 2007 (December)[3]
Lithuania 12.4 2012 (October)[11]
Luxembourg 5.1 2012 (October)[11]
Macau (China) 3.0 2010 (April)[77]
Macedonia 30.6 2012[78]
Malaysia 3.0 2011 (October)[79]
Mali 30.0 2004[3]

Malta 6.6 2012 (October)[11]

Marshall Islands 30.9 1999[80]

Mauritania 30.0 2008[3]

Mauritius 8.4 2010 (Q1)[81]

Mayotte (France) 25.4 2005[3]

Mexico 5.12 2012 (November)[82][83][84]

Federated States of Micronesia 22.0 2000[85]

Moldova 9.1 2010 (Q1)[86]

Monaco 0.0 2011[3]

Mongolia 12.2 2010 (Q1)[87]

Montenegro 13.24 2012 (November)[88]

Montserrat (United Kingdom) 6.0 1998[3]

Morocco 10.0 2010 (Q1)[89][90]

Mozambique 60.0 2009

Namibia 51.2 2008[3]

Nauru 90.0 2004[3]

Nepal 46.0 2008[3]

Netherlands 8.2 2013 (April)[91]

Netherlands Antilles (Netherlands) 10.0 2008[92]

New Caledonia (France) 17.1 2004[3]

New Zealand 7.3 2013 (January)[93]

Nicaragua 5.9 2009[3]

Nigeria 23.9 2009 (March)[94]

North Korea 0 2012 (April)[3]

Northern Mariana Islands (United States) 11.2 2010[3]

Norway 3.0 2012 (September)[11]

Niue 10.7 2006[95]

Pakistan 5.7 2010[96]

Palau 4.2 2005[3]

Panama 5.6 2011[97]

Papua New Guinea 1.8 2004[3]

Paraguay 7.9 2009[3]

Peru 5.8 2012 (January)[98]

Philippines 7.0 2012 (July)[99]

Poland 10.6 2013 (January)[100]

Portugal 17.7 2013 (April)

Puerto Rico (United States) 14.2 2013 (March)[101]

Qatar 0.5 2009[3]

Republic of China (Taiwan) 4.07 2013 (April)[102]

Romania 6.9 2012 (October)[11]

Russia 6.4 2012 (January)[103]

Saint Helena (United Kingdom) 14.0 1998[3]
Saint Kitts and Nevis 5.1 2006[104]
Saint Lucia 15.7 2006[105]
Saint Pierre and Miquelon (France) 10.3 1999[3]
Saint Vincent and the Grenadines 18.0 2009 (June)[51]
San Marino 3.1 2008[3]
Saudi Arabia 10.8 (males only) 2010[106]
Senegal 48.0;[citation needed] 30% among adults aged 24 and under[107] 2007
Serbia 22.4 2012 (October)[108]
Singapore 1.9 2011 (March)[109]
Slovakia 14.5 2013 (April)[11]
Slovenia 10.2 2013 (April)[11]
South Africa 25.5 2012 (Q3)[110]
South Korea 2.9 2012 (October)
Spain 27.2 2013 (Q1)[11][111]
Sri Lanka 4.2 2012 (Q1)[112]
Sudan 18.7 2002[3]
Suriname 9.5 2004[3]

Swaziland 40.6 2007[113]
Sweden 8.4 2013 (April)[11]
Switzerland 3.1 2012 (April)[114]
Syria 9.2 2009[3]
Tajikistan 60.0 2008 (August)[115]
Thailand 0.56 2013 (January)[116]
The Bahamas 12.6 2009
(September)[117]
Tonga 1.1 2006[118]
Trinidad and Tobago 5.8 2009 (Q3)[20]
Tunisia 13.3 2009[119]
Turkey 8.1 2012 (August)[11]
Turkmenistan 70.0 2008
(November)[120]
Turks and Caicos Islands 5.4 2007[121]
Ukraine 9.2 2009 (December)[20]
United Arab Emirates 4.3 2010[122]
United Kingdom 7.9 2013 (April)[123]
United States 7.5 2013 (April)
Uruguay 5.3 2012 (January)[124]
Uzbekistan 8.0 2008 (December)[125]
Vanuatu 78.21 1999[126]
Venezuela 7.7 2013 (March)[127]
Vietnam 2.9 2009 (April)[3]

U.S. Virgin Islands (United States) 13.3 2013 (March)[128]

Wallis and Futuna (France) 12.2 2008[129]

West Bank 17.2 2010[130]

Yemen 35.0 2009 (June)[131]

Zambia 16.0 2005[132]

Zimbabwe 70 2011[133]

CHAPTER EIGHT

June 6, 2013

F. Michael Kelleher,
Special Assistant to the President
Director of Presidential
Correspondence

President Obama/Council of Economic
Advisers:

We are obsessed with the index
provided by GDP—is it up, is it down—
to measure the health of the
economy—but have no such "alarm"
index when it comes to
unemployment....

For instance, the definition of "Full
Employment" is all over the map
among economists—from zero [Job
Guarantee] to 9%--with the former

based on anybody willing to work, should be guaranteed a job....

But ignored, at present, is that FULL EMPLOYMENT IS A PRO-MARKET CONCEPT—and thus an index regarding unemployment to measure the health of an economy is equally as important as GDP.

And while our number crunchers will hang on every digit, with the release of the Labor Department's May Jobs Report June 7, 2013—the fact is, the health of our economy is measured by a tread down....rather than an index that sets off alarms anytime our joblessness exceeds 3% [we have the legal authority to limit our unemployment to 3%, but inexplicably ignore this law!].

Our economy is only about ONE species...us, us human beings...any yet our economy does not factor in the HUMAN RIGHT to be a productive human being—and thus we, as a society, have an obligation to step in to address this HUMAN RIGHT.

We have an index to measure the status of our economy by how much stock we have left in our warehouses....etc.,....

And, our economic lexicon should include, for instance, an index such as PALR [Percent Above Legal Right]—or PAL for short, that would tag the percent our unemployment is over 3%--for instance, at 7.5%--our PAL Index would be 2.5, or two and one-half times over what is should be in a healthy economy.

Most importantly, this would bring unemployment front and center in a measure of the health of our economy—rather, than it being a step-child—and our policies would change to:

Fix unemployment, and this will fix the market—rather than the other way around---i.e., the failed path we are on now that will take until 2017, per the CBO, to get back to even an anemic 5.5% unemployment rate—and our unemployment benefits long since expired!

In short, the path we are on now is ANTI-MARKET, while claiming to be pro-market, our current policies actually HARM OUR ECONOMY!

See Also: ECONOMIC INCLUSIVISM, on Amazon/Kindle

Jim Green, Democrat opponent to Lamar Smith for Congress, 2000

CHAPTER NINE

THE FAIL-SAFE ELECTRONIC VOTING ACT:

So long as the potential for manipulation of electronic voting continues to exist—our elections in America will be in peril! In spite of all the polls showing a strong Obama victory--it was not until 10PM Central on 11-4-08.....that we could breath a sigh of relief....we had been cheated out of the past two elections....with many believing that Bush was never legally elected president of the United States....and we were braced for the worst.......this can, and MUST be fixed before 2010, so that this never happens again, and in the interest of all who support fair and open elections-- regardless of party. Accordingly, it is urged that we adopt the following proposed "FAIL-SAFE ELECTRONIC VOTING ACT":

THE FAIL-SAFE ELECTRONIC VOTING ACT

1) EVERY electronic voting machine (hereafter EVM), must be inexpensive, identical throughout the U.S. in a 1/150 ratio, and *must count and produce a hard-copy of the recorded votes*. In addition, an extra copy of their recorded votes would be produced (not necessarily a hard-copy), marked "Voter's Copy", and containing "NOTICE: Do Not Destroy Until Every Election On Your Ballot Is Certified". [If Wal-Mart handed us a piece of paper with the words "trust us" as a receipt for our purchases—we would be outraged—and this is our current electronic voting nightmare—but in this case it is our democracy at risk]!

2) *After confirming that their votes are recorded correctly*, the voter would then insert the hard-copy ballot into a software-free (count only) optical scanner (hereafter OS), for a second count. The hard-copy ballot would be retained by election officials in the event a candidate asks for a recount (*<u>not possible under the current system, and which undermines the legality of each such election</u>*). The EVM and the OS must be manufactured by different companies (which is universally true today).

3) Election officials assigned to oversee the EVM, would be prevented by law from overseeing the OS, and vice-versa, and stiff criminal penalties would be imposed for violations.

4) Further, every EVM would be programmed with raw data re the total registration rolls, by party, and norms

for their voting history, etc.,----as an "alert" to a possible irregularity, such as an "Under-vote"—or "vote-flipping" etc., and _standards_ established to suspend certification where there is an "improbable result", at least temporarily, of a particular election until the discrepancy is cleared up. (This is what computers do best, and it would be very easy to create such a program).

5) At the end of the election day, tallies would be taken from the EVM and the OS, for each candidate. _If the tallies didn't balance for any given election, or if there is an "alert", that election cannot be certified until the "error" is corrected._ If the candidates agree (the victory is certain), minor discrepancies in the count could be disregarded. While probably rare, the Voter, or a random sample of Voters, would be required by law to return their Copy of

the recorded votes to the election office to clear up any "error", or where an "alert" signals the need for same.

6) Further, every state provides for a recount when the total vote falls below a certain percent of difference between the candidates, impossible to conduct with the current EVM—and thus Congress must mandate the following regarding presidential candidates: A RUN-OFF election is mandated and triggered in those states where the percent of total vote is less than .5% of difference between any given candidates; said election to be held on the second Saturday following the election, on PAPER BALLOTS ONLY, and contain ONLY the names of the relevant candidates, for instance: "Barack Obama, Democrat" and "John McCain, Republican"—with oversight in counting by a representative(s) of each party—said

procedure providing more than adequate time to meet the Electoral College mandate. NOTE: Had this been the law in 2000, Al Gore would be our president, and the American economy would not be in meltdown!

7) Finally, absent the above safeguards, and until these safeguards are in place--Congress must mandate that PAPER BALLOTS, ONLY, can be used in our presidential elections. This is not a "partisan" issue, it is a "pro-democracy" issue. Most importantly, this will return the responsibility for our elections, and our vote counting, back into the hands of the individual voter, where it belongs, and out of the hands of "corporate control"---*it is after all "our democracy", itself, that is at risk if we don't take these steps--- and in that regard, is there any time or cost differential that is too great?*

Jim Green

CHAPTER TEN

Editor/NYTimes/Council of Economic Advisers:

From the first day we set foot in an automobile, let's say age 16—until our last breath—let's say age 80—if we are legal—we pay for and are covered by auto insurance.

A tiny, tiny handful complain—most don't—and like Social Security Insurance—most like being covered if they become disabled, or when they retire-—and on almost identical formats—the two share in common: We pool our money to protect us if/when fate taps us on the shoulder—

But have you ever heard of our auto insurance being called an "entitlement"?

So why is Social Security Insurance called an "entitlement"—with the inference that it is a government "give away program"? Pull up a chair....

It all started in 1935—and as true today, as then, the Republicans in Congress hate Social Security—

It raises the question, do they hate old people, do they hate the disabled, do they hate everybody?

And the way the Republicans in Congress vote against almost every issue that benefits the 99% of us Americans [as opposed to voting for what benefits the 1%]—it is the latter!

Indeed, the Republicans in Congress in 1935 wanted to remove the "old age" benefit from Social Security Insurance—which would make the law worthless!

Fast forward over the next, now almost 80 years—[in the 1950's President Eisenhower added "disability" to Social Security Insurance]—and without question it is the most successful social program in the 20th Century!

And yet, we still have Republicans in Congress, today, who want to destroy Social Security [i.e., the Ryan budget]—and we can now add "stupid on to "evil" for the bottom-feeders in Congress that have signed on to Ryan's budget:

Because were it not for Social Security moneys percolating up through our economy during the meltdown of 2008—we would not be talking about having narrowly averted another Great Depression—we would be buried in one!

There is no rational justification for the black-hearted Republicans in Congress who want to undermine Social Security—which brings us to why right-wing lunatics, in the 1970's, came up with the derisive and fraudulent term "entitlement":

They wanted to trick our ignorant and uninformed into believing it is a "government give away program"— when, in fact, it brings in more money than it pays out—is solvent to 2037 [the most solvent insurance program in America]—and like ALL insurance-- it is subject to actuarial adjustments from time to time—So What!

See: OUR GREED AND IGNORANCE, on Amazon/Kindle

Jim Green, Democrat opponent to Lamar Smith, 2000

CHAPTER ELEVEN

I HAVE included the following in almost all of my books, because I believe it has over-arching implications in our analysis of America, today, and would assert that where we went off the rails is the "human" belief that "sex is a sin"—and we took a very "natural and healthy" part of our life, and made it "dirty and nasty"—the following sums it up this dilemma.....

[I couldn't resist including this...and yes I am the author.....]

A MESSAGE FROM GOD

MANY CENTURIES AGO, a man of the cloth, we don't know his name, and in a flash of insight (perhaps induced by peyote) told his flock that "sex is a sin". And lo and behold he learned that by taking a very natural and healthy part of our life and turning it into something that was "dirty and nasty", that he could imprison his flock, and fill his coffers, and hallelujah it was a great day for the Lord!

Quickly, his miracle spread to other churches in his village, and then to the next village, and then the next county, and then state, and soon it spread to all the churches in the ancient world, and all of their flocks cowed in fear and shame and became imprisoned, and their coffers over-floweth. Hallelujah, it was a great day for the Lord!

And to keep the myth alive they started inventing stories, half-baked stories, that made no sense to anyone who is rational, such as "Mary was a virgin"—well, she just had to be a virgin because she would never partake in anything that was dirty and nasty, like sex (if you're doing it right), and this was necessary to make "sex is a sin" make sense...so they invented a Mary that was "sinless"--you get the picture. And their coffers over-floweth. Hallelujah, it was a great day for the Lord!

No one seemed to be bothered that when we play tricks on the human mind by taking something that is very natural and healthy, such as sex, and make it dirty and nasty that all kinds of bad things happen to the human mind:

Such as most pedophiles, and most serial killers, and voting Republican, and unwarranted suicides, and most mental illness, and unwanted pregnancies. (Teens not wanting to have sex is the perversion, not the other way around, and by replacing sex education and condoms, with unrealistic "abstinence", and by using blather about "low self-esteem" to shame them into not "sinning"—We have a teen pregnancy in the U.S. twice that of England and Canada!).

But none of this mattered, because their coffers over-floweth, and Hallelujah, it is a great day for the Lord!

There is a cure--------Tell these right-wing loonies to shove it....

GOD

ABOUT THE AUTHOR: I was employed in our Criminal Justice System for a cumulative 20 years as a probation officer, with 5 of those years as a chief probation officer. I authored the concept of "Shock Incarceration" which became law in Kansas in 1970, and then was adopted in numerous jurisdictions in the U.S. and also spread to Europe—it is currently identified in the U.S. as "Boot Camp" [as the means to "shock" the young offender—and a total distortion of my original intent—like many ideas, once released, they take on a life of their own]. I also instigated establishment of the first Court Psychiatric Clinic in the U.S., in conjunction with psychiatrists from the Menninger Foundation, as a chief probation officer. Finally, I was the Democrat candidate for Congress, District 21, TX, 2000. I would most define myself as a Social Ecologist-- [albeit my degree is in Psychology]. My web page is www.Inclusivism.org –which has been on the internet since 1996.

OTHER BOOKS BY THIS AUTHOR ON AMAZON/KINDLE/BN:

- **THE HARVARD BOYS CLUB: Hitler's Assault On Our Freedoms From His Grave**
- **MY LETTERS TO PRESIDENT OBAMA: Confessions Of A Compulsive Letter Writer**
- **OUR GREED AND IGNORANCE: Poses A Far Greater Danger To America, Than Terrorism**
- **LETTERS ON STEROIDS: Confessions Of A Compulsive Letter-To-The-Editor Writer**
- **THE FIRST TIME I HAD SEX: And, The Religious Intolerance Attack On America**
- **WHY PRESIDENT OBAMA LOST THE 2012 ELECTION: A Wake-Up Call**
- **ECONOMIC INCLUSIVISM: Neo-Capitalism/An Anthology—Inclusive**

pro-market solutions to our social problems

- AMERICA IS ONE SICK MF: Why Greed-Driven America Went Off The Rails....
  - EVERY GIVEN SUNDAY: A Scientific Formula To Predict NFL games
- IT IS IMPOSSIBLE TO BE A CHRISTIAN, AND VOTE REPUBLICAN: An Anthology

www.ingramcontent.com/pod-product-compliance
Lightning Source LLC
Chambersburg PA
CBHW071609170526
45166CB00003B/1032